T0167290

REGAIN YOUR
BALANCE

At Work, with Family, in Life

REGAIN YOUR
BALANCE

At Work, with Family, in Life

Identifying Your Goals and Ordering Your Priorities

Mark Sirkin, Ph.D.

REGAIN YOUR BALANCE: AT WORK,
WITH FAMILY, IN LIFE
IDENTIFYING YOUR GOALS AND
ORDERING YOUR PRIORITIES

iUniverse books may be ordered through booksellers or by contacting:

iUniverse
1663 Liberty Drive
Bloomington, IN 47403
www.iuniverse.com
1-800-Authors (1-800-288-4677)

Because of the dynamic nature of the Internet, any web addresses or links contained in this book may have changed since publication and may no longer be valid. The views expressed in this work are solely those of the author and do not necessarily reflect the views of the publisher, and the publisher hereby disclaims any responsibility for them.

Any people depicted in stock imagery provided by Thinkstock are models, and such images are being used for illustrative purposes only. Certain stock imagery © Thinkstock.

ISBN: 978-1-4917-7386-4 (sc)
ISBN: 978-1-4917-7385-7 (e)

Library of Congress Control Number: 2015918069

Print information available on the last page.

iUniverse rev. date: 12/22/2015

CONTENTS

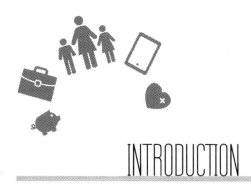

INTRODUCTION

The best and safest thing is to keep a balance in your life, acknowledge the great powers around us and in us. If you can do that, and live that way, you are really a wise man.

~ EURIPIDES ~

There was a time in the not-so-distant past when families were expected to give up everything in order to achieve the financial security they craved. Perhaps you remember those decades; perhaps you are too young to recall those times.

Those were the days when climbing the corporate ladder was a revered activity, and wives and children gazed fondly at pictures of the breadwinner in order to remember whether poor, exhausted Dad had blue eyes or brown. I remember one client during my consulting years, a vice-president in a Fortune 25 company, whose family, as a joke, printed a milk carton with his picture on it, with the words "Have you seen this man?" just as they did for missing children. It was funny and, at the same time, not so funny. He switched jobs a year or two later and travels much less than he used to.

Large companies moved employees from one city to another, like pawns on a chessboard. If you had any hope of climbing the ladder toward upper-management positions, you packed up the wife and kids and moved on from Chicago to Boston to New York to Tokyo.

In the intervening years, the divorce rate climbed. It was easy for fathers to lose touch with their families. Men died of heart attacks and strokes at an alarming rate; others retired, only to feel useless and unproductive.

Over the years, the identity of these men had become inextricably tied to their success on the job. New retirees found themselves wondering who they were and maybe noticed for the first time in a while that their spouses were no longer the people they married 25 or more years ago. And whatever happened to those darling kids who used to live in the house? Then women entered the workforce in earnest and joined the rat race.

Lest you think that this rat race has come to an end, look to the evidence of stress-related death and illness, the increase in the average number of hours worked per week by employees in the United States and around the world, and the skyrocketing number of divorces and children in single-parent families. And let us not forget those of us who are responsible for the care of aging parents.

We live in a world of conveniences that were designed to give us more leisure time, but it would seem that all the informational overload, whirring computers, and media blitz has given us is more time for work.

It is not unusual for men and women to work sixty or seventy hours per week on average. Some of us work eighty or ninety hours without batting an eyelash. And we fool ourselves into thinking we have a life!

If you are one of the enlightened few, you have already come to the conclusion that giving up a social and family life is too great a price to pay for a successful career. Maybe you have stress-related health problems, perhaps you are not eating right, and you are probably fighting with your spouse, significant other, or best friend because you spend too little time with the people you care about most.

You probably can't find the time to return phone calls or send a birthday card to your Aunt Betty. It doesn't matter if you are a lineman for a utility company, a pizza delivery person, a corporate executive, or an aspiring dancer.

In today's chaotic world, it is a safe bet that you don't have enough time for work, family, and friends. And, because your boss (or perhaps your clients if you are self-employed) holds a tight rein on your paycheck, it is likely that your family and friends are the ones who suffer.

So why this book and why now? I have been an applied psychologist for over 30 years, trying to bring psychological science into the real world. For some of those years, I was an academic, teaching and doing research on issues related to healthy and dysfunctional minds. But for most of that time, I was an organizational consultant or management psychologist, applying psychological theory and research to the world of business. In that capacity, I worked with more than one international consulting firm and also maintained an independent practice. I have worked with high level executives in Fortune 500 companies, family business owners with high net worth, and partners in professional service firms. My areas of expertise included executive development and coaching, team building, assessment, and strategic and career planning. I have seen first-hand the sacrifices and trade-offs that successful executives must make to achieve their goals; I have seen what happens when they can't, or won't, change. In addition, I have been witness to the incursion of technology in the workplace, from ERPs (enterprise resource planning software) to PDAs (personal digital assistants) and smartphones. Not that this is all bad, productivity has soared. But there has been a human cost and much of it is in the area of work/life balance. The executives and CEOs whom I coach struggle with high level business strategy, but also with mundane issues like "How can I run this meeting and get to my kids' soccer games?" or "My clients and partners expect me to be available 24/7 but my wife thinks when we are on vacation I should not be checking in with the office." This book is for my clients, and the millions like them throughout the world, who must juggle many demands on their time while still trying to live fulfilling personal and professional lives.

1
REGAIN YOUR BALANCE

We need to maintain a proper balance in our life by allocating the time we have. There are occasions where saying "No" is the best time management practice there is.

~ CATHERINE PULSIFER ~

Did you know that the Society for Human Resource Management has reported that 76 percent of American workers are considering looking for another job? Further, they estimate there will be 22 million new jobs created over the next ten years, but only 17 million new workers will be available to fill these jobs (www.shrm.org).

While every generation of workers has a different set of work expectations, the desire for work/life balance has become one of the foremost goals of every generation in the workforce today.

Baby boomers are reducing work hours, and many thirty-somethings are starting their own businesses in order to have more control over their lives and schedules. A recent study done by the Families and Work Institute illustrates that young workers just starting out in the workforce are choosing to turn down promotional opportunities to achieve greater work/life balance. And young people entering the workforce are not looking to re-create the hectic, no-time-for-anything lives their parents had. They want time to do everything that's important to them, including work, family, and friends.

Why do you suppose these apple-cheeked, enthusiastic job entrants might take this approach? In a study done with young employees by Families and Workplace, work/life balance was among the top priority for both genders (www.familiesandwork.org).

Most of these young adults were raised in families where both parents worked, and they experienced the sacrifice and demands placed upon their parents first-hand. Not surprisingly, of all the generations in the workforce today, these young adults are the most likely to consider job flexibility and schedules when they look for a job. That same flexibility is key to employee retention for companies that employ these young workers. The point of all of this background information is to let you know that you are not alone in your desire to find balance.

Today, all generations, in all types of jobs are looking for balance, less stress, and more time with family and friends. Like you, these people are willing to give it their all when they are at work. They expect to work hard, but in exchange, they want a life.

In essence, *find balance in your life*!

Let's begin with the idea that you once had work/life balance, but you lost it somewhere along the way. When you were a child, playing was your work. You didn't dread getting up in the morning, hoping for a few more minutes of sleep before you got out of bed. No, you eagerly enjoyed—even looked forward to—an active, exciting day. What happened? What does that imbalance cost you?

If you think that the balance between work and family life is a small problem, you may be interested to know that in addition to the few companies that have recognized the issue and taken the lead in establishing life balance programs, there are numerous organizations, foundations, universities, and groups doing research on this topic. Organizations as diverse as religious groups, government agencies, human resource companies, and behavioral scientists now study these issues. They do this not just because it is the right thing to do but because it impacts the bottom line in ways that are obvious and subtle.

There are real economic advantages to companies that recognize the need for life balance and create a working environment to help their employees live their lives more fully. Companies spend a lot of money training and keeping employees, and happy employees will stay longer, live longer, and contribute to the company longer. Plus, they are good ambassadors for the company and its products or services. And being ranked among the best places to work is something many businesses seek, because they understand the relationship between satisfied workers and productivity and profit.

The truth is we are just scratching the surface in understanding the true human toll that an unbalanced life takes. Many have studied the evolving societal issues and their roots in overwork and lost community connections.

If you *want* more balance in your life but you wonder whether it is all that important, let's talk about the reasons you *need* this balance.

As Aaron Antonovsky, a sociologist who specialized in the relationships between stress and health, has stated:

> We are coming to understand health not as the absence of disease, but rather as the process by which individuals maintain their sense of coherence (i.e. sense that life is comprehensible, manageable, and meaningful) and ability to function in the face of changes in themselves and their relationships with their environment (p. 27)

This phenomenon has many names: resilience, work/life balance, mental health, life satisfaction, salutogenisis, etc. The point is that it is certainly more than just having a job or making money; it is more than having a family or being involved in the community. It is a complex interaction of all of these activities where no one of them dominates the other for too long.

Health. Living an unbalanced life where work dominates can significantly affect your health. Long or stressful work hours can cause problems with your heart, your blood pressure, and your sleep cycles, not to mention your sex life.

Studies show a significant increase in heart attacks and strokes since the advent of the seventy-hour workweek. Long hours at work and lots of work-related travel also encourage poor diet and leave little time for exercise. The ironic thing is that as we become more out of shape, sleep less, and experience more health problems, we are no longer powerful assets to our employers. For the same reasons, we can also no longer participate fully in a family and social life. The irony is that the very things that caused us to make unhealthy decisions in the first place lead us to become less successful in those endeavors when we become ill.

Emotional Wellness. Your ability to give back to your family, friends, and community, as well as your own emotional stability, depends on a balanced life.

As overly dramatic as it sounds, you are likely to experience emotional problems, need counseling, and suffer from anxiety attacks or other problems if you don't have time to decompress and relax. This emotional toll also has physiological effects. On the other hand, there are numerous scientific studies on the benefits of relaxation, recreation, and meditation, *and these benefits are both physical and emotional.* You can't be ready to take on the issues in your family and support your spouse, parents, siblings, children, and friends if you have no emotional stamina.

If you've spent all of your focus and attention on work and find yourself so tired at the end of the day that you don't even want to talk to your family, you have a problem.

The societal impact of "all work and no play" has damaged and destroyed many a family, and the divorce rate continues to climb. Children grow up barely knowing their parents because they are away at work all the time. The term "helicopter parenting" has been coined for the recent phenomenon of parents who swoop in to attend school activities or birthday parties only to "fly back" to work and other responsibilities.

Family vacations, at least those lasting a full week or two, are certainly on the endangered list if not extinct. Vacations end up postponed, and many employees find themselves losing their accrued vacation time because they have rolled it over for so many years and just *not* taken the vacation they deserved. Statistics show that Americans are at the bottom of the international ladder when it comes to maximizing vacation time. And it's easier for us to justify because "everyone" we work with doesn't use all of his vacation time either.

Your emotional reserves are depleted. You have no patience with yourself or others. You are short on sleep and don't have the time or energy to make healthy food choices. Piece of pizza, anyone? It's all you have time for.

Is it any wonder that mental health professionals are busier than ever?

Stress. We have talked about the health implications related to a lifestyle that includes all work and no play, but stress is its own health factor.

Even if you like your job, if you have no time for anything else, stress will get you eventually.

We'll talk more about stress later, and you'll get some tips on how to eliminate or mitigate stress so that your body and mind will be better able to handle whatever comes your way. For now, what you need to understand is that stress can affect your physical and emotional health, and over time, it can make you very sick. If you are not in a position to change jobs or otherwise make a major change to relieve stress, you should at least learn how to handle it better. We're not talking about taking five years of classes here. We are talking about simple techniques you can use to help balance your life.

Remember that work/life balance is not just a question of the hours you spend in one place or another. It is also a question of how balanced you feel and how you react to things. The right balance is an individual choice, and what's right for you may not be right for someone else. And what was right for you at thirty may not be right for you at sixty. You will need to learn to pick up on the cues that tell you when you are in balance and then act appropriately to rebalance when the cues tell you to do so.

No matter how much time you have with your family and friends, you will enjoy it more if you are able to balance *yourself.*

If you can become less of a victim of stress and overwork and take control of your own reaction to stress, you will live longer, be healthier, and be happier at work and at home.

Family and Community. Government and university studies support the idea that the all-work-and-no-play lifestyle contributes to divorce, dysfunction in the family, and lack of involvement and investment in the community and neighborhood.

As the community grows apart and neighbors become strangers, emotional and family support for things like childcare, help with aging parents, and support following trauma and tragedy become real issues. The community turns to the government to supply services to fill this gap; as a result, taxes rise, and people remain strangers.

Families struggle with alternating and overbooked schedules, and children fail to thrive both emotionally and physically. Divorce is rampant, and single parents are under even more stress with even less time to pay attention to children. Things go from bad to worse.

Role models for marriage, relationships, and juggling time and family are important to a child's adult relationships. If we do not provide those positive role models, we perpetuate the problem. It is interesting to note that the youngest generation to join the workforce has started to rebel against jobs and employers that require ridiculous hours and dedication beyond the call of duty.

They understand the toll this type of career takes on a life. They grew up in families that suffered this impact. Perhaps our greatest hope for change lies in this generation of seasoned veterans of dysfunctional families.

Productivity. If your employer believes that your eighty-hour workweek is giving him more benefit, he should look at the statistics and information gathered by human resource consultants and companies that focus on efficiency and productivity.

It is a fact that the human brain needs downtime, rest, and recreation to recycle. Neuroscientists tell us that the brain uses 20 percent of all the energy we have available (Swaminathan, 2008). Work, worry, and stress all use energy that then becomes less available to analyze problems, deal with difficult people, or be creative. Think about your own life and the times when you had to work long hours to get something finished. Perhaps you found that you could barely focus after a certain number of hours. There is a reason that coaches who teach good study habits tell students not to cram for eighteen hours before an exam but rather to spread out the studying and mix in recreation.

Take a walk or talk with friends to regain your clarity and focus. If you and your employer truly want to take the best advantage of your time, you need to take time for yourself. If you do, you will spend less time reworking things you've done wrong, mistakes you've made, and details you've missed. And your employer will get better quality and output, regardless of your job.

Pilots are subject to time constraints and can only spend so many hours in the air, because airlines learned a long time ago that a tired and overworked pilot can make critical errors. In lengthy neurosurgery or heart surgery, surgeons take breaks and leave the operating room to clear their heads and rest. Again, these habits and techniques were learned the hard way. It was only after critical mistakes were made that these work policies changed. You wouldn't want a tired surgeon working on your open heart, would you?

Life Goals. Everyone has goals. And you are probably no exception. You may have work- and career-related goals that include promotions, expanded responsibilities, and recognition as an expert in your industry.

These goals are all fine, but be sure you don't just focus on your job. Many people come to identify their success in life by whatever positions they hold in their jobs and the recognition they get there. If they become disabled or sick, or if they retire, they suddenly find that they don't know themselves anymore.

These people don't have any identity outside of work, so they don't know who they are when they aren't working. They may have lost family and friends or have become strangers to these people, unaware of the important events that have happened at home while they were at work. This is one reason why these people often die soon after retirement; their life meaning was wrapped up in their work, and without that, they are lost.

To survive beyond retirement, or the cessation of work, people have to get to know themselves and their loved ones all over again. For some, this is an impossible task.

Be sure you set personal goals, family goals, and general goals in your life for growth and happiness. These goals should not be directly related to career or work, even if you set them while you are still working. Whether it is going on for a master's degree in the fine art you love, learning how to fly a plane, or playing the piano, you should have goals that keep you involved in other parts of your life. These activities should make you happy, stimulate your brain, and give you opportunities to socialize, give back to society, and feel good about yourself.

While you are setting goals, don't forget your family goals. Perhaps you have always wanted to take your wife to Hawaii. There may be grandchildren in the picture you want to set aside time to visit. Set the goal and a time table and do it!

Remember that life goals can include giving back to the community and to others.

It is interesting to note that because so many people cannot achieve their personal goals due to career obligations, we now find it difficult to get baseball coaches to volunteer their time or to get people to volunteer in hospitals and work for the community as a volunteer ambulance driver or firefighter. There is good evidence to show that giving back, or otherwise giving to others, is life enhancing on many levels. Every religious tradition encourages this—so now you have it from the highest authority!

2
MAKE CHANGES AND MOVE FORWARD

*People spend a lifetime searching for happiness;
looking for peace. They chase idle dreams, addic-
tions, religions, even other people, hoping to fill
the emptiness that plagues them. The irony is the
only place they ever needed to search was within.*

~ ROMANA L. ANDERSON ~

Now that we've discussed the reasons work/life balance is important and you know that others feel as you do, what do you do about the problem?

You may hate what has happened to your life, but you probably don't know how to change the landscape. You will be happy to know that you *can* change your life. Whether you make this decision to improve your health, strengthen a relationship, or simply gain control of your life, you have more than enough justification and motivation to make the move. However, you need to make a *firm commitment* to this change. Be realistic about how fast and how far you can go with this plan.

Before we go any further, let's be clear about something! We are *not* talking about quitting your job, moving to a pastoral setting, and hoping that someone will donate money to the cause. There is a real difference between achieving balance in your work and family life and the idea that you don't have to work at all.

Sigmund Freud said that work and love were the pillars of a successful life (Freud, 1962). Work is part of life, and it is healthy and constructive. It pays the bills; it gives us the reward of real accomplishment and a feeling of useful participation in the community and society.

What we are talking about here is the rational balance of your work life and social life—a balance that is all too rare in today's society. In fact, the absence of this balance has caused sky-high health-care costs and a dramatic increase in stress, including psychological and relational problems.

Now that we are clear on the goals and reasons for work/life balance, let's continue. If you've decided to jump off the merry-go-round and seek some occasional solace with your family and friends, you must have a plan for your escape.

First and foremost, you must set goals! Involve your boss, coworkers, friends, and family in the process. Keep the lines of communication open, and you'll end up where you want to be.

Sounds easy, doesn't it?

Depending on your age and how long you have run the rat race, you may find it harder than you thought it would be to achieve a good work/life balance, but with perseverance and the right support network, you can succeed. But first, be aware of your own attitudes. Different races, genders, cultures, and even age cohorts have different attitudes about work, family, and leisure time. If you are one of those people who just accepted what you were told—for example, fathers always work, mothers must stay home with children, idleness is the devil's workshop—then you may need to begin by questioning these received values. Downtime is not idleness, fathers can parent children, and mothers can work outside the home. Give yourself permission to think outside the box and do things differently than what you were told. Every generation needs to reinvent this balance for itself. Every generation has its own unique opportunities and challenges, so the text from your parents' or grandparents' generation won't always work for you.

Before cars, work and commuting were rarely factors in the work/life balance equation. Working from home was not even an option before computers. But these technologies can be liberating, enabling us to be productive from home after dinner or get onto that conference call with Mumbai at seven o'clock in the morning without even stepping onto an airplane.

It all just requires a little planning. Are you ready? Good! Then, without further ado, let's proceed!

3
PRIORITIZE WORK *AND* FAMILY

We need to maintain a proper balance in our life by allocating the time we have. There are occasions where saying "no" is the best time management practice there is.

~ Catherine Pulsifier ~

Before you decide to tell your boss that you simply must have more time off to spend with the family, you'll need to consider a few things.

First, most large companies now support balanced life plans; in other words, they recognize the need for their employees to take vacations, have time off to go to the doctor with a sick child, and get home for dinner at a reasonable hour.

But let's face it: in some companies, that commitment is lip service only. In other words, what the human resource policies say is one thing, while the reality is quite something else. In smaller companies, where the boss works alongside you, all bets are off. It's not that they don't care about these issues, but these companies tend to run by the boss's or owner's whim as opposed to by the policy manual. This is not to say that small companies are abusive. In fact, the data suggest just the opposite: smaller, family-owned companies are more satisfying places to work for the simple reason that they often feel like families. People willingly chip in to get things done, and if you need to leave to attend a child's sporting event, management at a smaller company may even understand more than the management at a large workplace.

But smaller companies, while perhaps more in touch with their workers' personal lives, are not subject to the same laws that govern larger companies. For example, some companies are so small that they are not subject to government regulations regarding hours, but it is important for you to understand that in today's world, no company in the United States can abuse an employee by working him 24/7. *Remember, there are labor laws to protect you.*

The first thing you need to do is to understand your rights. If you live in a country other than the United States, you will have to look at local labor laws to determine what you can expect when you go to talk to your boss.

Remember, the better prepared you are, the better chance you will have at getting what you need. If your boss does not know the law, you'll need to be prepared to educate her. Before you begin to execute your plan to balance your life, you'll want to think carefully about your job and your career goals.

You'll find some thought-provoking considerations below. Think carefully about each of these things; if you have items that are specific to your own job, add your own considerations to the list. If you really want balance and change in your life, you have to plan for it and then carefully execute the plan with dedication and persistence.

Here are some things to consider:

- Are you a member of a union? If so, there are rules regarding your work hours that must be enforced. You can talk to a union steward to get help with this.

- Do you have a contract that requires you to work certain hours? If you do, you may have to change jobs to get the balance you want in your life.

- If you are in a position that is critical to the company—in other words, no one else can do what you do—then you may be out of luck when it comes to getting reduced hours. On the other hand, if your contribution is mission critical to the company, you may have some leverage.

- Are you highly compensated (mid-six figures or above)? If you are, your hours may not be negotiable. Your boss certainly expects you to earn your salary, and the generous compensation is meant to reward you for the hours and stress. Again, you may have to change jobs and, at the same time, change your salary expectation. And don't forget: if you make a unique and valuable contribution, your employer may be willing to work with you.

🕐 Does everyone in your company and/or department work crazy hours? There are some jobs where you will not have the option to negotiate your departure time on certain days. But usually these jobs offer more flexibility when deadlines are not looming. Most workers expect an extra "push" around deadlines, but then they expect time demands to loosen up once the deadline has passed.

For example, when things are quiet and slow, you can ask your boss to let you leave early and/or get compensatory time to reward you for the crazy hours you are expected to work during an emergency.

Don't despair if you are a trauma nurse or work in emergency services or another job where you have to work really tough shifts. Many hospitals, fire departments, and other such organizations are now using a four-day on, three-day off rotation or other schedules that let these critical workers spend more time with their families. These flexible schedules also allow employees to schedule daytime appointments and decompress from the sometimes-stressful experiences and events that occur while they are on the job.

If your employer does not participate in these flexible schedules, perhaps you want to take your skills elsewhere. Or, you could try another tactic: educate your boss and company about these new, enlightened trends. Even though it is self-serving for you, changes in out-of-date policies will ultimately make the company more competitive in the war for talent.

Seasonal jobs may give you an opportunity to negotiate hours as well. Put your nose to the grindstone during Christmas hours in a retail store or summer hours in a surf shop, and ask for extra time off to reward your dedication during the off-season.

🕐 Look carefully at your position and determine if you have a job or a career. If you are in it for the long haul and hope to continue the climb to upper management, you can expect to work longer hours and endure a lot more stress.

Can you take another job in a lower-stress environment, perhaps at a company that prides itself on being family friendly, and still get into management? If you want to stay with your current company and continue to climb, and if your company is not dedicated to a balanced life for its employees, you may find it very difficult, if not impossible, to balance your life. On the other hand, as you are promoted into positions of power, you may be able to influence the company to move in a more positive direction on these matters. This is a long-term solution, however, that will probably benefit others more than you.

🕐 If your company does not recognize the need for and value of a balanced work and family approach, and if you are in a position to do so, consider going to your human resource department or manager and starting a grassroots movement to look at this issue.

Of course, management may immediately think you simply want to do less work than they want you to accomplish. To counter this, you'll need to arm yourself with information. There are all kinds of studies on increased productivity, employee retention, and performance that support the decision to create a balanced work and family environment.

Companies like DuPont, Motorola, Hewlett-Packard, Marriott International, Eddie Bauer, and many others have instituted these programs, and your employer may look to these leaders to get some ideas. Look into *Fortune's* Best Companies to Work For competition and see what innovators and leaders in the field are doing. These are the highest standards for which all companies should strive.

There are also resources available online for you and for your company. These resources include seminars for company employees and documents that teach managers and employees how to better manage time and workload so that the employee can accomplish more work and produce excellent output—all in less time.

Look at sites such as these:
> http://www.bc.edu/centers/cwf
> http://cwfr.la.psu.edu/research.htm
> http://www.wfcresources.com
> http://hrweb.mit.edu/worklife/index.html
> http://www.uml.edu/centers/CFWC

You'll notice that many of these sites are sponsored by universities, and these universities often participate with companies to help them execute a work/life balance strategy. In exchange, the university gains valuable insight and knowledge that it uses to advance its studies.

You will also notice that many of these sites have online or self-paced courses to walk management and/or employees through the process of planning for and executing a balanced work/life program.

If the reason you are working really long hours under tremendous stress is that your boss is a lunatic, then you need to change jobs (or at least bosses). But before you do that, you have to be honest with yourself.

Be sure that you aren't contributing to the problem and that you have honestly tried to improve your relationship. Be sure that you don't make things worse by offering to work longer hours or take someone else's shift because you feel guilty. If your attitude and feelings of obligation about work are contributing to your long hours and burying yourself in work you can never finish, you have to make some changes in your work habits. This may sound easy, but it isn't necessarily so. Many people function from guilt or a need to be liked by everyone, especially those in power. If this is your strategy, be honest with yourself and make sure it is working for you. Abusive or exploitative people rarely notice or acknowledge these extra efforts, and you may simply be working under a delusion of appreciation. If you have emotional needs that involve how much is enough or how to be well liked on the job, you will also need to address those.

Some companies offer job coaches, or life coaches, to help employees through these obstacles. If this is not an option through your employer, consider getting a life coach on your own time or go to a counselor and work through your issues.

Remember, it is important to do a good job and even, many times, to go the extra mile, but you should never put yourself in a position where you do all the work while other people are paid the same amount or more and receive promotions or time off when you do not.

If you have reached this point in your reading and are convinced that you would have to change companies and jobs in order to achieve the balance you desire, don't be discouraged. While you may think there are no companies out there that stress work/life balance, you would be surprised at the number of companies—both small and large—that are embracing this philosophy as a way to attract and retain good employees.

Companies as diverse as Colagate-Palmolive, Wegmans, and H&R Block have programs in place and report that their employees and managers have enthusiastically embraced work/life balance goals and priorities.

In many companies, employees are working together in teams, better than ever before, to ensure that the work flow continues when someone is away attending a child's kindergarten graduation or taking advantage of a four-day workweek to catch up on his golf game. As this trend continues and more companies are forced to consider this balanced environment to attract and keep valuable employees and skills, your search for the perfect company will become much easier.

In the meantime, look around.

These companies are much easier to find than they used to be, and it is more acceptable today to say that you want this balance—whether you are male or female, young or experienced, an executive or a retail clerk.

The last area we need to discuss in the work half of the work/life balance is time management.

Many studies show that the average worker does not feel he or she uses time productively. For example, 43% of Americans categorize themselves as disorganized, and 21% have missed vital work deadlines. Nearly half say disorganization causes them to work late at least two or more times each week (Bergen 2006). Or compare these findings from a 2005 Microsoft Survey: Most people actually use 60% or less of available work time. When more than 38,000 people in 200 countries were queried about individual productivity, it showed that even though they were physically at work five days a week, they were only productively using three days.

We can all learn to manage our time better in spite of the fact that there are more distractions than ever before. Following are a few simple tips to get your time under control. If you do these things, you will find that even in the most stressful and time-consuming jobs, you can reduce the hours you spend at work and arrive home in a less-stressed, more-family-friendly frame of mind!

Time and Organization Tips:

Make a To-Do List. When you have completed your list, put these items in order of importance, starting with the most critical. If you could only get one thing done today, what would be the most important? In addition, you may choose to lump these items into three categories: A) must do before the end of the day; B) should do by the end of the day (but may become an A priority tomorrow); C) important to start or attend to but not mission critical (yet). As you go down the list, you move from A items to B items to C items. If you find that Bs and Cs are consistently neglected, move them up to a higher priority category over time.

Cross the items off the list as you complete them and don't let yourself become distracted. Stay focused!

Since we all have interruptions, be sure that if you don't accomplish the items toward the bottom of your list, you add them to your list the next day so you don't drop them.

Use a daily planner or mobile app if that makes things easier. There are many programs to choose from, and most standard computer operating systems have planning functions that can be used to track tasks (these can often be found as part of a calendar or task management function).

Don't Waste Time. Use your spare minutes well. Take the train to work instead of driving and use that time to read critical reports you may have to review, or read your new equipment training manual on the bus on the way home. Alternatively, many people now use their commutes to catch up on phone calls (if driving) or emails (if riding) using their smartphones. Do be conscious of multitasking and safety issues, however; distracted drivers are often as dangerous as drunk drivers.

If you are going to take a break during the day and there is someone you have to see, stop by her office and grab her to go for coffee. Take that opportunity to talk about the issue and resolve it as part of your break. You'll feel like you took a break *and* got something accomplished at the same time.

Just Say No. If your boss wants you to work late on a day you have a family engagement, but you could work late the next night or come in early the following morning, suggest alternatives and see if those will work.

Don't be so quick to accept the request without probing to find out if there is another way to handle the situation. One busy attorney I know never missed a child's soccer game and rarely missed a family dinner. However, there were often times when he would go back to the office or log on to the computer late at night to finish his work.

If a coworker asks you to lunch but you *must* finish a report by three o'clock, politely decline the invitation.

Suggest that you get together for dinner or coffee later instead and then get your report done. That way, you don't have to give up the pleasurable experience, but you won't be stressed out and working until nine o'clock with your boss standing over your shoulder bemoaning the delay.

If the project your boss dumps on your desk needs to be rushed but she already gave you something that must be completed by the end of the day, ask for clarification on priorities. Be honest and give your boss a reasonable projection of how long it will take to do both projects and whether you can do both. Don't just take the project on and then not finish the other task she gave you, or you will both be unhappy. Speak up!

Master Your Media; Don't Let It Master You. Deluged by e-mails? Friends texting you? Overwhelmed by Facebook, Twitter, and other social media? It is hard to remain focused if you are constantly bombarded by messages from colleagues, friends, and family. When you are trying to get something done, *turn off all your alerts*. Only check e-mails and messages at certain times during the day. Maybe this can be your reward for crossing something off your to-do list.

If some new, pressing business matter does come across your desk, try not to respond immediately. Add it to your to-do list (in category A, B, or C). This may seem like an extra step, but it will help you maintain a sense of control, and when you look over your list at the end of the day, you will understand better where your time went. Again, you are the master of your media (and your life, for that matter!), don't let your devices tell you what to do and when to do it.

Know Your Brain and Body Rhythms. Do you know what the circadian clock is? It's that little clock in your brain that controls when you feel the most awake and when you want to go to sleep. If you are a morning person, attack the most difficult problems in the morning when your brain is the sharpest. That way, you won't have to rework the problem the next day when you discover that the "afternoon you" made the wrong decision about the budget. Likewise, if your most productive time is after lunch or early evening, plan accordingly. Clear the decks and turn off the incoming emails so you can be most productive during your productive time.

Get Enough Sleep and Eat Right. Your brain can operate on a short nap for a day, but if you are not sleeping enough, you will not think well or process information. As a result, you'll likely make mistakes and end up staying late to fix them.

Along with sleep, you should also consider the foods you eat. Foods high in sugar and carbohydrates will give you a quick rush, but you will soon crash and feel less energized. If possible, stick with foods higher in protein, which will give you longer-lasting energy. Also, foods low on the glycemic index contain slower-releasing carbohydrates, which can help you avoid the ups and downs of sugary foods.

Advertise Your Schedule. If you hate getting phone calls first thing in the morning before you've had a chance to organize your day and have your first cup of coffee, then let your calls go to voice mail until you feel ready to take the calls. You will be more focused and get more accomplished instead of having to say, "I'll have to get back to you on that," after hearing a ten-minute explanation of the latest crisis.

If you speak with someone regularly for reports or to coordinate work or schedules, let that person know your best times. Even go so far as to create a regular check-in time, whether it be daily or weekly, that works for you and your schedule.

Be Your Own Master. Sit down with a pencil and paper or a calendar and figure out when your free time is. Schedule and plan your activities at work and get your personal and family obligations on the calendar. *Treat these personal obligations with the same respect you would treat a business meeting.*

Don't automatically cancel personal appointments unless it is a real work emergency. In cases when you *must* cancel, reschedule immediately and apologize to your friend or family member. Explain what is happening, so your loved one doesn't think he is unimportant to you. And be sure to keep the appointment you make with that person the next time!

Don't Procrastinate or Agonize. Don't spend time during a family dinner worrying about the presentation you'll be giving tomorrow. Since you are not giving either your full attention, you will wind up doing both badly. Put your mind back where it belongs. Worrying never helped anyone accomplish a goal.

If you are prepared for the presentation, just do it. If you aren't prepared, make some time to help yourself feel more confident by getting up a little earlier or finding a quiet corner after dinner to go over things. By scheduling in prep time, you are also scheduling downtime (the time you are not spending preparing), which will help you be more relaxed and focused in the long run.

A little worry or anxiety is good; it gets you ready to make your best effort. But too much can be debilitating.

Don't procrastinate because you don't like a particular activity. One strategy is to *first* do those things you dislike the most and then reward yourself by doing the things you most like to do.

Put things on the calendar and stick to the dates—don't talk yourself into waiting, or you will just have more to do the following day.

Train and Delegate. Don't tell yourself you don't have the time to show someone else how to do a job that you *really* don't have to do.

This is one of the biggest errors that I see new managers and business owners make. Yes, it may be true that no one where you work can do a certain task as well as you. But there is only one of you and only twenty-four hours in a day. Take the time to teach your people, and soon you will have a well-oiled team machine going with all members doing what they are capable of doing.

Don't worry that other employees will take your job or your customers. If you create a functioning team with everyone performing well, your reputation as a manager, mentor, and coach will give you a shot at achieving the success you desire. With a track record for getting things done and a reputation for empowering team members, people will want to work with you. People innately want to do a job well and want additional responsibility. No one wants to be micromanaged, but people do need clear instructions and to know what they will be held accountable for. Welcome questions so that when people don't know what to do, they will feel comfortable asking you. In turn, you will have security that they know what they are doing.

And, when you don't have to do *all* the work yourself, you will find a lot more time to get those other tasks done and still get out of the office, shop, or store on time to get home for Mom's birthday dinner.

The other benefit to this time-management technique is that when you go on vacation or take that long-awaited three-day weekend to go skiing, you will not have to call the office every hour to be sure there isn't some problem you have to solve. Your family will greatly appreciate having your attention on a dedicated basis for a few days of much-needed bonding.

And don't overlook job-sharing programs and cross-training as concepts that will nicely cover responsibilities and ensure that the company keeps running when you are not there.

Get Organized. It is impossible to manage your schedule if you can't find things or if you have to re-create work or reinvent something because you lost it.

Take that action (to-do) list to heart; starting today, put a task at the top of the list to organize files or rearrange the store or inventory so it is easier to stock or find things. Also, when it comes to action plans, or to-do lists, there is most definitely "an app for that." Many of us have been integrating smartphones into our lives and will continue to do so. This is one good way to take advantage of that smartphone: use it to keep your to-do list handy and update it regularly.

Once you have things organized, don't let them get out of control again. The only way to justify the work involved in that reorganization is if you *know* you will never have to go through it again!

Keep a Realistic Perspective. Setting unrealistic goals is a mistake whether it is the completion date of a software project or the time you think it will take to deliver that report to your manager. If you underestimate the time required to get the work done, you will end up working late or even rushing to finish at the last minute—that is, if you make the deadline at all. Be realistic about when you plan to complete tasks and do your homework to be sure that you can accomplish the task in this time frame. Consider other ways to get the job done if you think these considerations will help you meet the deadline faster, but don't promise what you can't deliver. It is good to set goals that challenge you, but if you can't reach the goal, you will not do yourself any favors.

We'll talk about your goals and what you really want in a little while, but for right now, you need to think realistically about your dedication to a balanced life. You may have to make some sacrifices in certain areas, but you will reap many benefits too, including better health, stronger relationships, and greater life satisfaction, just to name a few.

Is balancing your work and your family life important enough for you to make some tough choices? If it isn't, you may not get the balance you want.

Decide *now*! Start *today*!

4
RECONNECT WITH HOME AND FAMILY

When people go to work, they shouldn't have to
leave their hearts at home.

~ BETTY BENDER ~

We've talked about the work environment and some of the
considerations there. Now it's time to open the Pandora's
box and talk about your family situation. Unless you are
starting your career fresh, with no history, you probably
have a lot of fence mending to do.

Your family and friends may be very discouraged and
disappointed that you haven't already found a way to balance your life and spend more time with them. If this is
the case, you need to talk to your family and friends and
tell them what you have in mind. Tell them that you are
going to strive to achieve balance in your life and ask them
for their opinions.

Remember, you don't have to take every suggestion given
to you. It's also important to make clear that although

you want thoughts from others on the topic, in the end you will do what you feel is best. Remember that you are not just gathering data; this is a first step to inviting those you care about in to participate more in your life and vice versa. Just by asking the question, you are sending a strong message.

Listen carefully and be honest with yourself and with your friends and family about what you can expect to achieve.

Don't promise what you can't deliver.

If there are going to be issues on which you must compromise or if you will have to look for another job where you will make less money in order to achieve your goals, be sure they understand that sacrifice and your reasoning behind it.

There shouldn't be any surprises. Before you start this discussion with others, put some thoughts of your own on paper and think through what you can achieve, realistically. Be prepared to talk to your family and friends and have some idea of how you will execute your plan. When they see how much thought you have put into it, they will take you more seriously too.

You can change this plan and work with your family to adjust it, but you need to go in with *some* plan or you will face a chaotic mix of accusation, opinion, and emotion. Here are some websites to get you started. After you look at these websites, you may have other questions and ideas.

Keep track of these. Write everything down so you can address all the issues with your boss and your family.

- *Boston College's Center for Work and Family*
  http://www.bc.edu/content/bc/centers/cwf.html
- *Forbes: "Best Companies for Work-Life Balance"*
  http://www.forbes.com/sites/
  kathryndill/2014/07/29/
  the-best-companies-for-work-life-balance
- *WebMD: "5 Tips for Better Work Life Balance"*
  http://www.webmd.com/health-insurance/
  protect-health-13/balance-life
- *Questia Online Library for Work and Family*
  http://www.questia.com/library/sociology-and-
  anthropology/relationships-and-the-
  family/family/work-and-family.
  jsp?CRID=work_and_family&OFFID
  =se1&KEY=work_family&LID=14582939
- *WorkLife Balance.com*
  http://www.worklifebalance.com
- *Bella Online*
  http://www.bellaonline.com/site/workandfamily

If you do your homework online, you'll find many websites in addition to these that may be useful to you.

There are sites that target working women's issues (Bella Online), sites that specifically target stress at work (WebMD), and many other topic-specific sites to help you deal with your job and your family in a way that makes life easier for the ones you love. There are even sites that discuss best practices in the workplace that can help you arm yourself for that ultimate discussion with your boss or human resources department (Forbes).

When you come up with some ideas to discuss with your family, be sure you preface your discussion by explaining that you want to change your focus and balance. Tell them that you know work has been pulling you away and you want to fix that. Just knowing that you recognize the problem and want to work on it will make them feel better.

If you have children, talk to your spouse or significant other before you call a family meeting. Consider how you want to address this with the kids. Remember that children will often take what you say very literally, so don't play fast and loose with your language. Think carefully about what you want to say and the words you will use and only promise them what you can deliver. Of course, you may need to adjust your language to make it age appropriate; keep the concepts simpler for younger children who may not understand the demands of work and the type of time juggling that most grown-ups do.

Don't lead your children to think you are quitting your job to stay home with them and play all day—unless you've just won the lottery, of course!

It is likely that whatever plan you put into place to regain some balance in your life will take some time to execute, so don't promise that everything will be fixed immediately. Change will take some time, especially if you have decided to switch jobs or careers. As you get ready for these changes, you may have to cut back on expensive purchases and other luxuries. Children may not fully understand all of this, but the effort you take to explain it will go a long way. Be sure everyone is on board before you pull away from the dock! Make sure your children understand how important this is to them and to you and what they will get in return.

As you make your plans for better work/life balance, consider these things:

- You may be trading long hours for financial stress if you are going to take a job for less pay. How will that impact the family and your commitment to this process? Can you find ways to offset some of the impact of this financial decision?

- If you are not changing jobs but you are going to manage your schedule in a different way, how will your family schedule change to accommodate that?

- Can you eat dinner a bit later so you can eat together as a family? Can you take the children to an early movie to spend time with them before you take that afternoon shift?

- If you and your spouse work different shifts to be home with the children, include time in your plan for the two of you to get together. If you have to set a specific date to do that, don't be shy about it.

- Find creative ways to spend time with your significant other. Can you share a cup of coffee in between shifts? Get up a little earlier? Go to bed a little later? Don't neglect that most important person in your life.

- Whatever your schedule is, find some quiet time for yourself and quiet time with your family without the TV playing in the background. Eat dinner together or play a game. When you go grocery shopping with the children, take a break and go to the back of the store for a cup of coffee and a doughnut. The kids will appreciate the time with you, and it will make the shopping more tolerable. Find time to do something as a family at least once a week. Order a pizza so you don't have to cook and spend time playing a board game or taking a hike.

- Pick an activity that everyone likes and just do it! It sounds corny, but even a few minutes of this kind of activity will help you feel that you have a lot more balance in your life.

Assuming you have done what you need to do to find more time away from work or change jobs, you may think you've now completed the transition. However, that is far from the truth. The fact is that balancing work and family—in short, balancing your life—can be a lifelong challenge. Remember, there are lots of distractions, and that extra time you've carved out of your work schedule will not do your friends and family much good if you spend it parked in front of the TV or computer instead of with the ones you love.

Two traits will help you immensely, but they will require some work: self-discipline and awareness. Most of us suffer from the absence of both of these traits, but if you focus on them and on breaking bad habits that distract you and take you away from what you really want to do, you will be much happier.

First, let's talk about self-discipline. The absence of this trait is what gets you off track. It is what pulls you to the computer game instead of out to the backyard to play a game of catch with your children. It is what makes you put off those chores and tasks—whether they are related to home or work—that then spring full grown at eight o'clock in the evening to remind you that you must complete them before morning. And you spend another evening in the den or office crunching numbers for bills or finishing that project you put off instead of tucking your daughter into bed or visiting with your husband over a glass of wine.

When you catch yourself listening to the news anchor while your wife tries, in vain, to tell you about her day, make the decision to reach for the remote and turn off the TV. Self-discipline and breaking old habits go hand in hand. If you've gotten used to becoming a vegetable when you get home from work, it won't matter how much extra time you get with your family.

This is one reason prioritization and time management were emphasized in the previous chapter. These things encourage habits that reinforce this discipline. Although not every conversation and movement needs to be scheduled, having a sense of the flow of your day and where gaps of spare time may be will help increase your feelings of relaxation and self-control.

Distraction vs. Awareness

Mindful awareness is a special way of paying attention. It often involves a calm focusing of attention, without the desires or urgencies that sometimes accompany our thoughts. Become aware of what you are doing and saying, and every time you catch yourself taking things for granted, remember that the little time you have with your family and friends is important. As the cartoonist Walt Kelly says in his Pogo comic strip:, "We have met the enemy, and he is us." In this case, the enemy is what many call multitasking.

Multitasking is the fantasy that we can do several things at once and equally well. In a recent psychological study, there was good news and bad news: About 2.5% of subjects can multitask without performing worse at either task, in controlled studies. These are being dubbed "supertaskers" (Watson & Strayer, 2010). So the good news is that you may just be one of the elite 2.5%. But let's face it, the odds are that you are probably part of the vast majority, 97.5%, that isn't quite so skilled at doing two or more things at once. The problem is simple because, for most of us, the brain processes information sequentially, and although it is very quick and allows you to jump from thing to thing, make no mistake: unless you are an elite "supertasker," a distracted brain is a less efficient brain. So if you are okay with doing several things badly, go right ahead. But if you are trying to do a quality job, whether it is attending to someone's conversation or going over a spreadsheet, give each your full attention and stop the pretense of multitasking.

Listen to what your friend, spouse, or child is saying to you.

Listen to your father when he calls you on the phone and wants to tell you about the fish he caught. Look for opportunities to grab a special moment with loved ones during the chaos of your week. Don't just slide through life. Be mindful, be connected. For a fuller discussion on how to simply be with someone and listen in a mindful manner, read Jon Kabat-Zinn (2009) or Ron Siegel (2009) to learn about mindfulness practices especially with other people as your focus.

Put down the smartphone; it makes you dumb!

The smartphone has changed many lives for the better. I'm not sure I could survive anymore without one, but it is important to realize there are trade-offs. Have you watched young people (or even older people now) at dinner? Conversation often comes to a standstill while everyone attends to his smartphone and the constant stream of information coming through it. Let's face it; you are not really paying attention to your dinner company if you are constantly checking your phone or tweeting or posting on Facebook. Even if the other person says she doesn't mind, it detracts from the quality of the relationship. And as you become more disciplined about this and start paying more attention to those around you, you may find that you object when other people do this too. Don't be afraid to speak up, but don't be a hypocrite. You need to change first.

Make it happen!

There are two additional things you may want to consider in your quest for balance at home: communication and rules. These two things will give you more balance and engender better relationships.

The first consideration is *rules!*

Perhaps you are thinking that you hate rules. Most people do, but they are a necessary part of life. Think of rules as a way to manage expectations and make life more predictable for everyone. Neuroscience shows that our brains crave predictability (Kahneman, 2011). Rules in your work/life balance will give you and your family structure. When the rules are bent or broken, the exceptions must be carefully explained.

You and your family must know that you are serious about these changes. In order to reinforce this, the rules should only be bent or broken when there are extenuating circumstances.

Rules are never ignored, even when exceptions are made.

Rules should not only apply to when and how the family will get together but to things like whether your child can stay out late on a school night, whether children are expected to attend a family birthday party, or whether smartphones and the texting that goes with them are allowed at the table.

Rules also apply to *you* as they relate to when you'll come home from work and whether you will attend the Friday night movie with the family or beg off and say you have to work. How often will you make it to the league soccer game or the lacrosse games?

Rules are for everyone.

A good way to establish these rules is to have the family sit down together and develop the list. Everyone can vote, and everyone's opinion counts. Some rules may be very simple, and some may be temporary. And if you have a set of rules printed or typed on your refrigerator, you and your family will feel more confident in your balance and will know better what to expect when specific situations arise.

It's important to remember that you shouldn't expect the family to obey the rules if you don't obey them. You have to keep your end of the bargain too!

The second consideration is *communication!*

To keep your life and the life of your family in balance, you need time and attention. But you also need communication. Even if your job is demanding, you can balance your life more effectively by communicating better with the family. Your job and what you do when you are away from home on business should not be a mystery. If you have to go out of town, tell the family where you are going, when you will be back, and why you are going. While you are gone, use phone calls, e-mail, and text messaging to keep in touch so they don't feel like you are on another planet.

If you say you are going to call at a certain time, be sure to do so. Don't leave them hanging. Leave silly notes or messages for them to find while you are away and bring home little gifts. You don't have to bring anything expensive—for example, some kids get a kick out of the small ketchup bottles that come with your room service order. That is easy and inexpensive, and it lets them know you are thinking about them.

If you can have dinner together at night, do so, and keep the conversation pleasant. Don't choose dinnertime to bring up bad grades or that boyfriend you can't stand. Your kids will not want to have dinner with you if you do that.

Make the mealtime conversation pleasant, and keep the distractions out of the dining room—no TV, music, or other disruptions. And as mentioned earlier, try to keep smartphones off the table (my kids used to hide them in their laps!) and texting to a minimum or verboten altogether.

Family meetings are a great way to keep the lines of communication open. Once again, remember that everyone's opinion counts and everyone gets the floor to speak. Of course, different ages will be able to participate in different ways. Don't let the older kids bully the younger ones or vice versa. Not only are you teaching them a skill (how to participate in a group discussion), but you are teaching them respect for each other and for others' thoughts and feelings.

Keep the meetings constructive and informative and talk about whatever is going on in your lives. A twenty-minute family meeting will give you a chance to touch base and feel connected. Even if you are working long hours, you will not feel like a stranger in your own home. Some families may prefer to do this at dinner, while others may want a separate time and place. It is the quality of the discussion itself, not necessarily where and when it is held, that is most important.

Agree on how and when you will communicate throughout the day, even when you are not home. Is your child expected to call you and check in when he gets home from football practice? If she goes to a friend's house, what are the rules about letting you know and when to come home?

Create a mail slot or an in-box for all the notices from school, permission slips, and other items. A mailbox for each person in the family is even better if you have the room. Then, you can leave little notes for each other to keep in touch or just to say hello or I love you. This is also a creative use of text messaging. Just a quick text to say "Hope you're having a good day." or to ask "How's it going?" is a powerful message that lets someone know you care.

5
FRIENDS ARE THE FABRIC
OF YOUR SOCIAL LIFE

The love of family and the admiration of friends is
much more important than wealth and privilege.
~ CHARLES KURALT ~

While we are on the subject of your personal life, let's not forget your friends. Everyone has them, and everyone needs them.

Friends are a necessary social extension, and they provide an outlet, a group of like-minded people who share values, even though they may not always share every opinion. Time out with friends, whether old high school buddies or friends you've made at work, is important. A strong social network can literally save your life, or at least extend it. Research shows that people who have a good network of friends live longer than those who don't.

You can spend time with friends by enjoying a movie, the ballet or theater, a cup of coffee, an occasional dinner, or perhaps even sharing an activity you both like, such as bowling, golf, baseball, slot machines, or a book club. All of the techniques discussed for family life can also be applied to friends. Above all, keep in touch. Schedule events and get-togethers with a realistic eye to what you can achieve. And don't forget social networking, not as a substitute for a real-life visit, but as a way to keep in touch and an excuse to pick up the telephone or pay a visit when you see some news about someone you care about.

Many people work long hours, have demanding jobs, and still manage to participate in monthly groups or scheduled activities. These fun activities are a welcome relief from grueling work schedules.

Put social appointments on your calendar just as you would any business meeting and be dutiful about keeping the appointment even if it seems a guilty pleasure during that critical crunch season at work.

If you must cancel, communicate clearly with your friends and let them know why you have to reschedule. But *do* reschedule. Don't leave your next time out to chance, or you will never get together.

When you go out with friends, even if they are coworkers, use your newly learned skills in self-discipline to keep you out of the realm of work discussion. Try not to talk shop, or you will not get away from the stress you tried to leave behind at the office. However, it's important to realize that talking shop is not the same as talking about your profession or people you know in common. It is a hard habit to break, and it may take some time and focus to learn the new habit of general conversation. You can make it fun by agreeing that the person who breaks the don't-talk-shop code first will have to buy a round of drinks or has to pay for dinner.

You'd be amazed at how quickly your coworkers will learn the lesson!

If you have a friend or a group of old college chums with whom you love to socialize, try to pick a monthly or weekly date—the second Tuesday of every month, for example—and get together then. Everyone will look forward to these occasions, and you won't feel so deprived of social contact.

During times of high stress and long hours, take the time to go out for a walk, get a cup of coffee, or have lunch with someone outside the office. Get away from the people you see in the halls every day and enjoy a breath of fresh air.

You'll feel much better.

Don't give up the activities and friends you love. Exercise and socialization are key to balancing your life, and even though you may feel they can be postponed until a time when your career is not on high speed, your health will benefit from the short breaks and scheduled visits you insist on taking.

Something to consider is that if your friends have fallen by the wayside with the advent of your most recent and most hectic job, you need to get some new friends.

People do not live by work alone!

Although your family is very important to you, your friends serve a different purpose. They are often more honest with you, and they will forgive and forget without the same intimate emotional attachment of a spouse, parent, or sibling. You can count on friends to make you laugh and to be there so you can share your successes and failures. They are part of your psychological armor and a necessary part of your life's balance.

Seek out friends actively and don't be afraid to invite your new friend for a drink or coffee. There is no harm done if the friendship does not blossom. Friends make you more interesting, expand your horizons, and keep you from becoming a boring, all-work-and-no-play kind of person. Again, you have to be disciplined, have a plan, and pay attention in order to take advantage of these opportunities.

Many couples kill two birds with one stone by spending time together with other couples or mutual friends. They have quality time with each other and with people who are part of their social network. These relationships certainly qualify as both social time and family/significant-other time. Anytime you can combine social activities, such as spending time with friends, family, and your spouse, you should do it. However, don't do this at the exclusions of the other types of relationships.

A note about cross-sex friendships: In modern times, men and women socialize with each other all the time, but there are some hazards you should be aware of. More importantly, you need to at least be aware of your motives and those of your friend. If neither of you is married and the friendship turns into something more, that could be a good thing. On the other hand, if one or both of you is in a committed or married relationship, you need to be aware that there is the potential for a platonic relationship to become something more … complicated. In addition, your spouse or significant other may feel threatened or misunderstand the relationship. None of these are reasons not to be friends, simply reasons to be more aware of the ramifications.

Fear of jealousy may sometimes be a factor in how you spend your time. Jealous feelings are a natural part of the dance that couples do as they balance alone time, work time, social time, and family time. There is no right way or wrong way or simple rules to guide you. Every person, and therefore every couple, is different. Acknowledging feelings and communicating needs and intentions are the best ways to keep resentments from festering. For some couples, these can be dangerous waters, while for others, it's no big deal. Again, be considerate and respectful of those whom you care about.

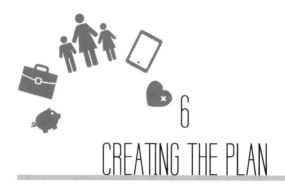

6
CREATING THE PLAN

Happiness is not a matter of intensity but of balance, order, rhythm and harmony.

~ Thomas Merton ~

Up until now, expectations have only been touched on, but they are perhaps the most important part of your balancing plan. Expectations come into play in several ways.

First, there are *your* expectations.

What is it that you expect to get from a more balanced life? More free time? A closer relationship with your spouse? The time to pursue an advanced degree? Maybe you want to learn to speak a new language, ride a horse, or build a webpage? Any or all of these things are fine goals, but your expectation to achieve balance must take into consideration that some of these goals will take *more* time away from your family.

In order to find balance in your life, the first thing you have to do is to get it straight in your own mind. What is balance for you?

Is it more time for yourself? More time for your family? Don't make a promise to get more work/life balance and then squander that balance with poor planning. What do you expect to achieve? How will this balance change your life? Are your expectations realistic for the planned time frame and actions you want to take, or are your dreams too ambitious for the time and energy you have to spend?

Satisfaction vs. Balance

Up to this point, the focus has been on the idea of balance, which is still the long-term goal. But for some, the term *balance* can be taken too literally. If by balance you really mean eight hours of work, eight hours of family/personal time, and eight hours of sleep, then you may never achieve that goal until retirement (and maybe not even then). Let's begin to think in terms of satisfaction rather than literal balance. Satisfaction comes from doing fulfilling work and other activities that are in line with your deepest values. Those values are your life compass, and you need to become more aware of what they are so they can guide you in the right direction. Once you have determined your own values and goals, use these to set your expectations. Next, you'll need to look to your employer and your family and friends to be sure that you understand and can meet their expectations and that those expectations are also in line with your deepest held values.

It is all well and good that you expect to regain some balance in your life, but if your employer still thinks you should work eighty hours per week, you aren't likely to get far. Put it on paper. Then talk to the people most important to you and those whose support is crucial—like your boss—to find out what *they* expect. Then compare notes and figure out if everything is aligned.

If it isn't, you'll have to adjust the plan. Once you get the plan right, you can move forward more quickly and with more success.

What is your true north?

We've been speaking about values without really saying what values are. This is a complex topic that has occupied philosophers, religious leaders, and the average person since the beginning of human self-reflection. What is the life worth living? How do we choose between two (or more) goods? This is not the book to discover what is important to you. Some people already know, while for others, it requires a conversation with a psychotherapist, spiritual leader, or significant other. At the end of the day, this book will mean little without a sense of what is important to you, and this is a question—some might even say *the* question—worth asking.

There has been some work in the field of psychology recently in the area of positive psychology. One of the best things to emerge from this work is a scholarly discussion of values and character strengths (Peterson & Seligman,

2004). In addition, a test or self-assessment has been created to help you assess the values most important or salient for you. The test is called VIA (for Values In Action), and at the time of this writing, the test can be taken online for free. To take the test, visit https://www.viacharacter.org and click the circle marked "Take the Free VIA Survey." .

Values are your personal compass. They are what get you excited about something and determine what is satisfying in your life versus what you have to do whether you want to or not. Without a sense of your values profile, whether arrived at through a test or self-reflection or a holy book, you won't know what is important to you or how to choose among competing goals and demands. In other words, whatever path you choose requires a destination, and your abiding values are your life's destination.

GETTING REAL, SETTING GOALS

You can't have a better tomorrow if you are thinking about yesterday all the time.

~ CHARLES F. KETTERING ~

Now, let's talk about goals. Like any other important life decision, you need to have goals, or you are shooting in the dark. As discussed in the last chapter, your goals are determined by your values, and your values are your personal compass.

To set goals for your work/life balance, you have to take your values and translate them into whatever it is you want to achieve. Be as specific as possible.

For example, if you are going to look for a new, less-demanding job, your goals might include the industry you want to work in, the type of job you want to get, and how much money you want to make, as well as when you want to get the job.

Here are some examples to get you started:

- My goal is to get a job with one of the top ten banks in the United States as a bank manager, by May of this year.
- Reduce the number of hours I work by ten hours per week in time for John's next Little League season.
- Visit my mother every Sunday for at least three hours.
- Train two to three people on my staff to take over the bookkeeping process by January of next year.
- Schedule and keep a weekly date with Mary for dinner and a movie.

Simple, right?

Remember, the best way to set goals is to word them simply but specifically. That way, you can measure your success without trying to guess whether you succeeded. Remember that your expectations and goals must be realistic, or you will never get to where you want to be.

The next task at hand is to figure out *how* to achieve your goals. For these tasks, SMART goals give you the what, when, and how.

Use SMART Goals:

- **S**pecific: be clear about what you are trying to accomplish.
- **Me**asureable: be able to measure or assess progress. How will you know when your goal has been reached?
- **A**chievable: goals that stretch you are okay, but impossible goals defeat the purpose.
- **R**ealistic: breaking the world record or being the richest person in the world are lofty goals, but unless you are one in 6 billion, try to keep it real.
- **T**ime-limited: make sure to set an end point, you should know when they are accomplished or not. Don't let things go on too long.

Now it is time to figure out just how realistic your expectations and goals are, because you have to establish a plan to achieve those goals.

Let's take the first example and see what we can do with that one:

> "My goal is to get a job with one of the top ten banks in the United States as a bank manager by May of this year.

To establish a workable plan for this goal, you would need to consider the following questions:

- What are the top ten banks in the United States?
- How do you find out what jobs are available at each bank?
- Are you qualified for the bank manager positions at these banks?
- Will these job openings require you to move your family to another location?
- Are there job placement agencies you can use to find these jobs and arrange for interviews?
- Do you have an up-to-date resume?
- Do you have the appropriate wardrobe for this job (or at least for the interviews)?
- Do you have good references?
- Does your family and/or spouse support this decision?
- Is it realistic to expect that you can research, find, and get this job by the date you set?

You can probably think of more questions you'll need to answer, but this list will give you some idea of the considerations involved in just one goal.

For every goal you set, you will have to think about how reasonable the goal is, how achievable it is, and exactly how you plan to accomplish it in the time frame you have set for yourself.

When it comes to the goals that involve your family and friends, the emotional attachments and desire to do the right thing may make it hard to think clearly and plan accurately for how and when these things will happen.

Be honest with yourself and with each other, and by all means, include your support network in setting your goals. Ask your family to come up with ideas about how you can accomplish these things. Brainstorm and leave the door open for crazy ideas. You'd be surprised at what you might uncover in this way.

Then sit down and pick through the plan and decide which ideas will work and which must be discarded.

As you start to execute your plan, be sure you review it occasionally to ensure that you are still on target and evaluate whether you have to change anything. Use interim goals, when appropriate, to help you track your progress and feel a sense of accomplishment. Interim goals are a helpful way to break down large goals into smaller, bite-size pieces. Large, aggressive, life-changing goals can be intimidating. But broken down, they are just a series of items on your to-do list. Consider the old riddle: how do you eat a cow? The answer is one bite at a time. So start with a large goal, and then break it down into smaller, more manageable SMART goals.

Don't overdo it. When I coach executives and we get to this part of the goal-setting process, I often have to urge them to limit the big goals to only three or four per year. That may seem like a small number, but let's think about this realistically. If you really want to create lifelong changes and it took you all these years to create the situation you are now dealing with, is it realistic to try to change everything at one time? Probably not. Two or three life-changing goals a year (or even a decade) is as much as most people can handle.

Life happens!

You may have to change some of your time tables and tasks to incorporate the unexpected changes in your life. For example, you may plan to take a job that pays less and gives you more time at home to help care for an aging parent. But if that parent requires some sort of catastrophic care or expensive medical treatment, you may have to keep the higher paying job to earn the money you need. If so, consider seeking out community support services and low-cost, high-quality caregivers who can come in and work a few hours every day so you can continue to work the longer hours to pay for the care. If this is not an option, do you have family members or friends who can pitch in for a little while until you figure out what to do next? Does the parent have a home that can be sold to help pay for the extra health-care costs?

Remember, there is always more than one way to solve a problem. Don't panic and don't give up on your work/life balance goals. Just find another way to accomplish them and be realistic about whether you can achieve them in the same time period. Perhaps you need to extend your time table a bit to accommodate the new developments in your life.

Being forced to rework your goals doesn't mean you won't get there. Just knowing you have a contingency plan will keep you afloat and moving forward.

8
COMMUNICATE FOR SUPPORT

> *The way we communicate with others and with ourselves ultimately determines the quality of our lives.*
>
> ~ ANTHONY ROBBINS ~

We talked a bit about communication when we discussed family issues, but here the topic is broader. In general, communication will help you balance life and work by establishing clear boundaries and expectations with others.

Communicate regularly with the people in your network.

Your network includes your manager, your friends, your family, and your coworkers.

First and foremost, don't assume that others know what is going on. Even if your secretary has a copy of your calendar on her computer, she may not have looked at it.

Spend a few minutes with your assistants, staff, or others each morning to be sure everyone is on the same page. Make sure everyone knows your schedule for the day, including when you will in the office and available and when you might be away at meetings. If you are leaving for a business trip, be sure you leave critical contact information so you don't have to wait until after you return to the office to address problems.

If you are responsible for delivering something—a report, a brief, a write-up, etc.—ask questions to be sure you know what has to be done, if there are preferred methods to accomplish the task, and when the task needs to be completed.

Don't leave things to chance.

If you do, your boss, colleague, or assistant may grab you on your way out the door and tell you that you have to stay and finish something. Unexpected things happen and crises come up, but planning reduces the chances that these unforeseen events will ruin your plans.

Communicate.

Exchange information with others and find out how they do things. You may learn a better or faster way to get things done, and as a result, you may be able to get out the door with fewer hours under your belt. Also, be aware of the people around you and the skills they demonstrate. If there is a colleague who consistently gets reports in early or projects under budget, you may have something to learn from her. Ask! Let her know you admire this tendency and then ask for her secret. Discussions over coffee or a drink may create a relaxed and accommodating atmosphere where you can learn something, exchange valuable information, and generally cement social bonds.

At home, be sure that all family members know the schedule, when they need to be home for family events, and what is expected of them. If everyone pitches in and understands his role, no one person will be stuck working at chores or doing homework, instead of having some fun family time together.

With friends, be clear about when you are free and be sure your friends understand that they have a place in your life and are important to you. Make dates, but let them know if these dates are subject to change because of late work hours.

Try to plan events when you don't have anything really pressing at work so you won't be distracted. If you have a calendar function on your computer or smartphone, use it!

You'll find that you get more enjoyment out of your time with friends.

If you have elder care issues, make sure you communicate often with your family. If you are expected to transport or help your parent or ailing uncle, get any doctors' appointment or engagements on your calendar. Be sure that everyone understands what is important to you—your values, priorities, and the things you are willing to put aside because of more critical issues. This will help your staff, family, and friends accommodate and change appointments if they see a conflict.

And never forget that communication is a two-way street. Be sure *you* understand the priorities of your boss, your friends, your coworkers, your spouse, your parents, and your children.

If you understand how others think and feel, you can offer to pitch in and help as needed. This is a favor they will gladly repay the next time *you* need help. Keep lists and information handy to offer if you have to leave work or home quickly and others need to know what has to be done. Keep copies of your schedule and itineraries handy when you travel, and always let others know where to reach you and when you will be back. Again, use calendar apps if you have them.

In meetings, use flip charts to capture thoughts and record agreements and team contracts so you don't waste time trying to figure out what the team decided later on. If you are in an office job that requires reporting, communicate through e-mail and written reports to be sure everyone knows the schedule, the action items, and who is responsible for what tasks. Taking these steps will save you time and trouble later.

Communication isn't just talking.

Most of what you'll learn and use to get things done comes from listening to what others are telling you. Whether you are in a meeting at work, talking to a co-worker in a retail store, or discussing the family vacation with a family member, practice active listening. Don't tune out. Test for understanding to be sure you actually heard what you thought you heard and interpreted it correctly.

Active listening is more than just nodding your head; it is repeating what you've heard, in your own words, to make sure that you heard correctly. This may feel redundant or like a waste of time, but it is truly surprising how often people mishear or misunderstand what has been said. The idea is not to repeat back, parrot-like, what someone has just said. The idea is to communicate back to them (the active part) what you heard them say (the listening part). Active listening is one of the most important skills that therapists, teachers, and managers can learn. There are many resources available to help you master these skills (e.g., Hoppe 2011 or Ferrari 2012).

If you possess these capabilities, you have a significant advantage in personal relationships. No matter how little time your family has together each day, if you are really talking to each other and listening to each other, you are a world ahead of your neighbors in maintaining balance in your life and in your relationships. In some sense, this is a variety of mindfulness, which we discussed earlier.

Think about it for just a moment: Balance is achieved through the focus and attention you place on a particular thing or person at a particular moment in time. Being present in the moment is all anyone can ever hope for, because life is simply a series of such moments strung together. If a person feels valued and important, if she feels that she has your full attention when you are with her, you are well on your way to achieving one of life's more elusive goals.

9

TIPPING THE BALANCE IN WORK AND LIFE

You will never find time for anything. If you want time you must make it.

~ CHARLES BUXTON ~

If you can't afford to make major changes in your career or your life in order to gain the balance you need and want, there are some other ways to decompress and capitalize on the time you *do* have for yourself and your family. If you institute some simple changes, you will *feel* like you have more time for yourself, and the time you have will be more rewarding.

Quality over quantity.

First, we should talk about making the time you already have available better. Many people who have studied and mastered work/life balance are busier than ever. The difference is that they know how to transition between work and social life so that they don't waste time in limbo, trying to shake off the worries of the day and, in the process, ignoring the time they *do* have with family members and friends.

Basically, it's all in the approach!

Don't let life run over you!

Get control. Know what you have to do and then get it done. This way, when it is time to transition from home to work or from work to home, you will be ready for the transition. To accomplish this, you'll want to think of your work time and your personal time' as existing in two different worlds. Each of these worlds requires different skills and a different focus, but they are both important.

You can use some of the ideas here to create a transition ritual for yourself—one that gets you out of one world and ready for another world.

For example, to go from home to work, you can try these things:

- Get things ready the night before. The less rattled you are going into the day, the less unbalanced you will feel throughout the day.
- Don't wait until the chaos of the morning to pack lunches, sign homework, or put files in your briefcase.
- Try to leave extra time in the morning to prepare for the unexpected.

- Set your alarm and get up on time so you don't have to rush. If you have kids, always allow enough time for that last-minute emergency. Children have a way of foiling the best-laid plans.

- You can try getting up before everyone else does if you think this might work for you. That will give you a little quiet time to get things done in peace before the rest of the house starts to stir. You will also be less likely to forget things in the rush. Some people use this extra quiet time to have a cup of coffee and write out their list for the day. Whatever works for you is fine.

- Be sure you don't run short on time to get to work. If you have young children, you have to be creative here. A good-bye routine is a good idea. Try something that is fun and easy for the kids to get into. Having a routine will make the drop-off at daycare a lot easier, and you will be out the door in no time. Kids like—and some psychologists might even say need—predictability at key transition points, like going to bed or leaving for school. This is where rituals come in: the good-night story, the hug-and-kiss good-bye, and other things that work for you and your family. Also, have a plan for what you will do if your child is sick or if you wake up to a foot of snow and you can't miss work.

These routines take a few tries to get right, so be patient with yourself and your children. As soon as they understand the routine, your kids will often take it from there.

You may even be able to make a game of it at certain points.

Focus on what fun things they might do that day or what they will learn. Emphasize how eager you will be to hear about what they did when you see them in the evening. And avoid the wrenching good-byes and feelings of loss.

Transitions are difficult, and this is why kids may choose to test the limits of your patience at the most inconvenient moments. Without realizing it, they may be setting you up for a test: what is more important, being on time for work or helping me find my homework? These are the times that test all parents. Some planning will help, but often, children will outwit the best-laid plans. There are no magic answers here; you have to roll with the punches and, most importantly, handle your own stress.

Use your trip to work—whether by train, car, or bus—to read (or listen to) a book you enjoy, make a list of action items for the day, have a cup of your favorite coffee, or listen to your favorite music or meditation CD. You'll need that sense of Zen and organization to get ready for the day, and you'll greet the problems of the day with a calm and focused approach.

At the end of the day, don't forget to transition back to your social world. Switch out of the work mindset and use your time in the car, train, or bus to reprogram yourself. Consciously leave behind the work worries, make a short list of items to remember for the next day if you need to do so, and then let it go.

Listen to your CDs or read your book and focus on your family and friends. Think about what you will do when you get home and about the things you will share with your family and what they might want to tell you.

Some people close the office door and meditate for a few minutes before they leave, or they use the very act of closing the door to close the door on the day, as they say.

Whatever works for you is fine!

One woman completes the transition by fixing her makeup, changing her shoes, and spraying a fresh scent of perfume in the bathroom on the way out of the office. Now, she's ready for the evening!

An advertising executive changes his clothes to casual clothing and sings along with his favorite country-and-western tunes on the ride home. He gets a lot of stares by passing drivers, but he loves it.

You may have noticed that firefighters and police officers never leave the station house in their uniforms at the end of their shifts. There are many reasons for that transition, but the psychological transition of taking off work clothes and putting on the street clothes is, nonetheless, a psychological transition that works for nurses, doctors, and firefighters alike.

For anyone who wears a uniform, a suit, or other clothing that they don't wear at home, the transition is something they don't have to explain. The mother who wears a business suit and high heels to work is a different person to her children when she changes back into her jeans and T-shirt at home.

Make much of the homecoming too!

Give hugs and kisses to all and announce your arrival. This will help you to transition, and it will give your family the boost they need in seeing you at the end of the day. And don't discount laughter as a means of transition from work to home. If you like to listen to stand-up comedians or talk to a funny friend on the train on the way home, do so. Laughter has a very positive effect on your brain and on your outlook on life.

Remember that coming home is not always a bed of roses.

Your spouse, children, or parents may have had a hard day. They will likely save their troubles to tell you, their trusted confidante. After a long, hard day at work, the last thing you may feel like doing is to listen to troubles.

It helps to take a breather.

The time-honored tradition of a cocktail or glass of wine will also help you to transition from your work self to your home self. Go change, take a shower, and relax for a few moments before you tackle the discussion about bills and health problems.

You can anticipate these discussions by calling home before you leave work to check in. Take the pulse of how things are going at home and find out who is having a bad day.

If you have to pick up your kids on the way home and you are trapped in the car with a bundle of upset or nervous energy, let them blow off steam and tell you their trials of the day for a few minutes. Then turn on some music they like, settle in, and agree that when you get home, everyone will take a deep breath and relax.

Reinforce that *home* is a soothing place—a place they can go to be with those who care about them and to get away from the problems of the day. If *you* have a really tough day, be honest with your family and ask for a few minutes to compose yourself before you join in the fray. Be sure that they know that they have done nothing wrong and that you are just taking the time for yourself because of the day you had at work.

As you practice some of these techniques, you are bound to come up with your own ideas and rituals. You should try them and make liberal use of those who work for you in order to help yourself with this transition.

10
STRESS MANAGEMENT

*The greatest weapon against stress is our ability
to choose one thought over another.*

~ William James ~

Perhaps the most pervasive and difficult problem to solve in life balancing is that of stress. Whether you are at work or at home, there is likely some stress in your life, and that stress can interfere with your enjoyment of your career and your social life.

Stress is what we experience when we must adjust to the constant and conflicting demands of our lives. If you like your job and work long hours, if you are very competitive and always trying to win, you may experience a more positive form of stress.

But for most of us, when we experience unremitting stress and we don't know how to handle it, it makes us angry, frustrated, irritable, depressed, and fatigued. We may get headaches, develop an ulcer, or suffer from insomnia. Unless we can learn to eliminate or mitigate stress, we will function poorly on the job, at home, and with friends.

Recognize that stress is real and can affect your health, your happiness, and your relationships. There are lots of ways to defeat stress, and you'll need to find the right one for yourself.

Here are some websites that will get you started:

- http://www.mindtools.com/smpage.html
- http://www.mayoclinic.org/healthy-living/ stress-management/basics/stress-basics/ hlv-20049495
- http://www.mindfullivingprograms.com/ whatMBSR.php

There are any number of other sites that focus on stress. Many of them are sponsored by universities and contain some great information and ideas about specific types of stress and stressful events.

Specific life stressors may have their origins in very different things. For example, if your boss is a major stressor in your life or if there is abuse or a hostile environment at work, you have a different problem than the stress that comes from financial troubles or from caring for an ailing parent, spouse, or child. But regardless of the cause of your stress, the effects are the same. Extreme stress can be short-lived, as in stress after the death of a loved one, or it can be long-term, such as a demanding job with no easy way out.

How and why stress figure into your work/life balance goals.

It is very simple. Whether you are trying to balance your time or simply improve the quality of your life, it is important to acknowledge stress and understand that there *is* something called positive stress and something called negative stress.

Positive stress is the stress you feel when you are planning your daughter's wedding or preparing to make an important presentation. You may be happy about the event and looking forward to the occasion, but that doesn't mean there is no stress involved. That kind of stress is not harmful and can be quite invigorating.

Negative stress, on the other hand, *is* harmful, especially if it occurs over a long period of time. Consider on-the-job stress or stress in a relationship because of poor communication or the absence of focused time spent with a loved one. All of these things can damage your health and the quality of your life.

Begin your journey to stress management by identifying the stressors in your life and looking for the places you feel most stressed. Next, address the source of the stress, if you can. The best way to approach stress is head-on. Later, we'll talk about how you can relieve and mitigate stress if you are in a situation where you cannot eliminate it altogether.

But first, let's look at how and when you can take charge and what you can change. As we said earlier, you have to start by identifying the stressor(s) and taking stock of your reactions to this stress.

Notice the emotional and physical responses you have to stress.

Do your muscles tense? Do you get headaches? Do you get nauseous or have stomach pain? Do you get nervous and irritable? Don't pretend it isn't an issue—just become aware. Be objective about your reactions. Chronic stress is insidious, in part, because it goes underground, so to speak and becomes subconscious. For that reason, it can lead to pain, dysfunction, or illness over time without many of us ever realizing that the pain we feel today is related to a stressor we have been exposed to over a long period of time. Becoming aware is the first step to becoming better.

Next, figure out what you can change and how you can relieve or eliminate the stress.

Can you take those things that cause you the most stress and schedule or spread them out so that you can tackle them when you are prepared and rested, rather than taking them on in a whirlwind with other things going on at the same time? Research suggests that one of the key ingredients in a stressful situation is the lack of predictability of when the stressor event will occur (Miller 1981; Lupien et al. 2009). If you can protect yourself from random stressors or find a way to put them off until a better time when you can give them your full attention, you will be better off. In one famous experiment, monkeys who were randomly stressed were much more likely to develop stress-related illness than those who could control when the stressful event occurred (Weiss 1968).

Can you shorten the time you are exposed to the stress?

If your boss is a great stressor in your life, don't schedule a one-hour meeting with her if you can avoid it. Instead, try stopping by her office to talk briefly, or if you must schedule time, schedule it during times of the day when you are less likely to feel harried. Also, work to keep the meetings short and to the point. Stay on track and don't get off on tangents that may make the situation more stressful.

If you have times of the day or situations where you are under a lot of stress, try to take a break. Walk outside for a few minutes or go to get coffee. Break the pattern and then come back refreshed to finish the task.

Focus on making changes to avoid the stress.

For example, extend your time tables to make a project more feasible or set more realistic goals. By doing this, you will hit the problem at its root cause instead of trying to run and catch up all the time.

Try to analyze and alter your reaction to stress.

Much of the damage done by stress is not done by the event itself but instead by your body's reaction to the event. Your body and mind perceive danger and react accordingly, causing everything to become exaggerated. The danger seems more threatening, the task more daunting, and the outcome more dismal. This is called the fight-or-flight reaction, and it is deeply programmed into your nervous system. This is where your powers of rational thinking can take back control. It is a classic technique that cognitive behavior therapists use. If you are overreacting to a stressor, use your mental powers to analyze what is going on and talk to yourself about a more reasonable reaction. You may feel powerless, but you are not!

Reason with yourself and ask, "What is the worst that can happen?"

Are you overreacting to the stressor and making your fear and emotional response worse? Is everything as critical and time-sensitive as you think, or are you just overly sensitive to pleasing everyone, all at the same time?

Don't obsess over the negative factors and predict failure.

Stick to the positive, and even if there are issues, focus on the things that worked well and note them. *Then* revisit the places that didn't work so well with a more objective eye toward improving the process and try not to place or take blame. Just be sure to learn from your experience, and the next time it will go better.

Remember that everyone makes mistakes!

Whatever you do, don't go into a project or situation predicting doom. You will never succeed that way, and in the process, you will endure the stress of trying to consider every what-if and failure in the book. There is power in what you think. Negative thinking and expectations make negative outcomes more likely. By the same token, positive thinking can lead to positive results. Either way, you create a self-fulfilling prophecy.

Learn how to mitigate stress by diffusing it when it happens.

When your heart starts to race and your palms get sweaty, take a two-minute time-out and try some deep, slow breathing. It will reduce your heart rate and bring your mind back into focus. Consciously relax the muscles in your shoulders and neck, around your jaw, and in your scalp. Unclench your hands and close your eyes. Do these things just for a moment. Sometimes counting your breaths, in and out, to ten and then starting over again is a helpful way to distract and refocus your mind.

Stress and your body.

First, prioritize taking care of yourself. Exercise three or four times a week. Cardiovascular workouts like aerobics, rapid walking, or running are great to relieve stress and strengthen your heart and lungs. Most physicians now recommend at least thirty minutes a day of simple walking. It's nothing special, but it provides most of the exercise you need and yields many physical and psychological benefits.

It's also crucial to eat healthy. Don't eat fast food. Try to eat a well-balanced diet, and avoid stress responses like smoking and drinking. Take frequent breaks. Remember, you can still think through problems and get things accomplished while you take a quick walk or go for a glass of water.

Maintain supportive friendships and relationships.

Don't let connections with those you care about die on the vine. It is this replenishment that will keep you going. Set your own goals, and don't let others force you into situations you don't like. There seems to be a consensus among scientists that our brains evolved to make us more social (Goleman 2006). We need other people, especially those whom we enjoy being around. Don't neglect these relationships! Another benefit of these connections is that friends can often help you find a new perspective or solve problems in ways you hadn't considered.

You will always have some stress and frustration, but if you know yourself and if you build your reserves to meet these challenges, you will lead a much more balanced life, and work stressors will not creep over into your personal life.

But what if you've done all the right things, and you still suffer the effects of stress? What if that stress is not something you can easily change? Remember, even if you can't change the stressor, you can change your reaction to the stress.

Sometimes just knowing you have to calm down doesn't help much. Exercise has been mentioned as a way to mitigate stress, but there are a lot of other structured approaches to mental and physical relaxation, from meditation and yoga to biofeedback. All of these are beneficial, so pick the one that works for you.

Here are a few ideas to get you started:

- **_Deep breathing_**, or learning to breathe deep into your abdomen and slow your body down, sounds easy, but it takes a bit of practice. This is the basis for many types of meditation.

  However, you can do it anywhere, even on a bus, train, or plane. Once you've learned the technique, you will wonder how you ever got along without it. Because the increased oxygenation of your blood brings more clarity to your brain, you will double the benefit by being able to solve problems better, as well.

- **_Biofeedback_** is a method of relaxation that helps you control your responses to and change how your body and mind react. Your brain learns how to adjust as you use monitoring equipment to track your heart rate, muscle tension, blood pressure, and skin temperature. The new equipment is so light and user-friendly—not at all like the old, clunky equipment from the past. A quick Internet search will show what is available. The range of equipment is varied, as are the prices, from less than a hundred dollars to several thousand dollars. You may have to do a little research, but it is worth it, as these are very powerful tools. Also, there are new smartphone apps appearing all the time for significantly less money. Don't forget to look into those as well.

- *Guided imagery* uses affirmations and relaxing images to calm and focus your mind and body while controlling your breathing so you are more relaxed. It is easy to learn, and the more you practice, the better and faster your brain will respond to the cues, putting you into a state of relaxation more quickly every time.

- *Meditation*, sometimes called *mindfulness* (see above), has become one of the most popular techniques to achieve relaxation. It is not necessarily tied to any religious belief and can be learned alone through self-study or in groups. Meditation changes your brain waves and alters the response to stress in your mind, your emotions, and your body.

You can start and end your day with a brief meditation, and eventually, you may find it so helpful that you will employ this technique wherever you are, whenever you feel stress. Combine deep breathing with mindfulness meditation by following a deep breath from your nose down into your lower abdomen, and then let it out slowly. This is also called belly breathing, and it is our natural, relaxed state. This is the way babies breathe.

Among its many negative effects, stress also fools us into breathing incorrectly (from the chest), which only makes things worse.

- *Focused muscle relaxation* teaches the student to tighten and relax groups of muscles in turn until the entire body is in a state of relaxation. It is easy to learn and can be mastered quickly and effectively with good results.

- *Yoga* is an ancient form of exercise from India that is based on the connection between the muscles and organs in the body, breathing techniques, and the combined effects on the mind. The goal of yogic practice is to restore balance to the body and your emotions through postures, stretching, and breathing exercises.

- *Tai Chi*, sometimes spelled *Taiqi*, is another ancient practice from China. In Tai Chi, the practitioner, or player, learns relaxed, graceful movements that emphasize flow, balance, and the connection between mind and body. One can memorize an entire form that may take twenty minutes from beginning to end or just learn and repeat a short set of movements or exercises. A related practice is called ***Chi Kung***, sometimes spelled *Qigong*, which is also very popular in China. These are breathing and simple movement exercises that are relaxing and invigorating.

Other forms of exercise, such as cardiovascular workouts, running, and walking, will increase the release of certain good chemicals in your brain, thereby relieving stress, frustration, and anger and helping you to sleep.

If you suffer from stress-related insomnia, you should consider trying one or more of the solutions outlined here. It will help you get the sleep you need to function well and to keep you healthy and balanced.

Work at relaxing, and you will be relaxed at work—and at home.

11

A LIFE WORTH LIVING

> *Balance, peace, and joy are the fruit of a success-*
> *ful life. It starts with recognizing your talents and*
> *finding ways to serve others by using them.*
>
> ~ Thomas Kinkade ~

As with any plan, your plan for work/life balance must be kept fresh and flexible. Be sure you allow for contingencies and guard against backsliding.

Old habits die hard, and you may find yourself in need of a refresher to stay on track.

Look at your plan often and keep talking about it with your friends, family, and coworkers. The more you reinforce its importance to yourself and others, the less chance you will fall back into your old ways. Remember that nothing ever goes just as planned, so be ready for the unexpected and don't let it throw you off course or get you down.

If your plan did not include a contingency for a particular event, just sit down, look over the plan again, and make room for some new ideas to address the problem you face.

Don't be discouraged if you hit a snag.

Remember that it will take awhile for the world to catch up to you, and while many companies and people may not understand the need for balance, the fact that you do may save your life and your relationships.

If those around you fail to recognize the importance of your efforts and scoff at your decision to take a lower-paying job or choosing to stay home with a sick child, remain secure in the knowledge that you are running a marathon, not a sprint. In the end, you will finish the race well. Remember to stay grounded in your values; they are your touchstone.

You may be breaking new ground. You may be a role model, and that position is not always easy. Pioneers have hard work to do, but they *are* the first to see the beauty of the new horizon. So, stick to your plan! You will get better at this as your old habits change. Remember to exercise self-discipline and have the courage of your convictions.

Remember to pay attention to the important things and keep things in perspective. Don't spin your wheels or expend too much energy on the things you can't change or the things you don't feel are important.

Just because someone else tells you it is important, doesn't mean you have to believe them. Keep the plan and the perspective fresh and if one thing doesn't work, try another. It is your commitment to the change that is important.

And if you find another way to get there, that is just fine! It may not turn out exactly as you expected, but your focus on the goal of balance is the important thing. Without that focus, you can't change anything!

Don't be afraid to get advice from others you trust if you get stuck on the path. You don't have to do this alone.

12
SUMMARY

There are only two ways to live your life. One is as though nothing is a miracle. The other is as though everything is a miracle.

~ ALBERT EINSTEIN ~

We've covered a lot of ground in a short period of time, and you may want to review this information again to make sure you've got it all. The concepts are simple, and although you may find yourself wondering if all of them relate to work/life balance, you will find answers as you implement the steps we've outlined here.

Each of these steps is designed to address a different part of the challenge of achieving work/life balance. Having enough time and focus to appreciate your life outside of work is one thing. Having the mental, emotional, and physical stamina to do it all is another. It is also important to understand how to keep your life in balance and know what factors are involved in a long-term commitment.

If you can't manage your time, you will never have enough of it, no matter how few hours you work in a week. It will also be important to take a step back to look at how you got to where you are and what issues you'll need to resolve.

Think of this book as a primer, of sorts. Of course, the particulars are yours to figure out. Your specific issues are different than the issues your neighbor will face, but there are many common factors.

As we said at the beginning of this discussion, you'll need a plan, so let's review some of the key components. You can adjust and tweak your plan along the way as you need to make changes, but getting the plan in place is the first and most critical step.

- Sit down with a pencil and paper or at your computer and gather your thoughts and expectations.
- Talk to your family, your boss, your coworkers, and your friends and get their thoughts.
- Then set your goals!
- Make the plan and move forward.
- Adjust the plan along the way if you need to do so, and be realistic about what you can accomplish and how long it will take.
- Keep the lines of communication open and keep people informed about your goals, your progress, and what is important to you.
- Learn to manage your time better so you can leverage the free time you have to use it as you wish.

- Schedule and keep commitments with your family and friends.
- Find ways to improve your productivity and learn to transition from work to home and back again so that you are truly present in every situation and not spinning your wheels thinking about other things.
- Don't get distracted, stay focused on the task at hand.
- Use self-discipline and stay committed. Pay attention and listen to others. Do things, especially mundane activities, right the first time so you don't have to do them over again.
- Learn to handle and diffuse stress and eliminate it from your life wherever you can.
- Be optimistic and positive.
- Exercise your mind and body by finding a practice that's right for you.
- Understand that work/life balance is key to your health and happiness. It can actually make you more productive at work and give you a better quality of time with your family and friends.

And so we come to the end of our journey; now it's your turn to get the plan on paper.

You can do this, many have. It's a process that takes time, training, and attitude adjustment. Take control of your life and live it to the fullest. Remember to keep your priorities and values straight.

One last thing to remember: You don't live to work—you work to live!

> *Don't be afraid your life will end; be afraid that it will never begin.*
>
> ~ GRACE HANSEN ~

REFERENCES FOR REGAIN YOUR BALANCE

Antonovsky, Aaron. *Unraveling the Mystery of Health: How People Manage Stress and Stay Well*. San Francisco: Jossey-Bass, 1987.

Bergen, Jane Von "So many reasons to neaten up...", Boston Globe 3/12/2006 (Esselte survey by David Lewis).

Ferrari, Bernard T. *Power Listening: Mastering the Most Critical Business Skill of All*. New York: Portfolio-Penguin, 2012.

Freud, Sigmund, and James Strachey. *The Standard Edition of the Complete Psychological Works of Sigmund Freud*. London: Hogarth Press, 1962.

Goleman, Daniel. *Social Intelligence: The New Science of Human Relationships*. New York: Bantam Dell Publishing, 2006.

Hoppe, Michael H. *Active Listening: Improve Your Ability to Listen and Lead*. Hoboken, NJ: Pfeiffer-Wiley, 2011.

Kabat-Zinn, John. *Wherever You Go, There You Are: Mindfulness Meditation In Everyday Life*. New York: Hachette Book Group, 2009.

Kahneman, Daniel. *Thinking, Fast and Slow*. New York: Farrar, Straus, Giroux, 2011.

Lupien, Sonia J, Bruce S. McEwen, Megan R. Gunnar & Christine Heim. "Effects Of Stress Throughout The Lifespan On The Brain, Behavior And Cognition." *Nature Reviews Neuroscience* 10 (June 2009), 434-445.

Microsoft Survey, March 15, 2005

Miller, Suzanne M. "Predictability and Human Stress: Toward a Clarification of Evidence and Theory." In *Advances in Experimental Social Psychology, Vol. 14* (Leonard Brooks, Ed.). New York: Academic Press, 1981.

Peterson, Christopher & Martin Seligman. *Character Strengths and Virtues: A Handbook and Classification*. Washington DC: American Psychological Association / Oxford University Press, 2004.

Siegel, Ronald D. *The Mindfulness Solution: Everyday Practices for Everyday Problems*. New York: The Guilford Press, 2009.

Swaminathan, Nikhil. "Why Does the Brain Need So Much Power?" *Scientific American* 29 Apr. 2008.

Watson, Jason &, David L Strayer. Supertaskers: Profiles in extraordinary multitasking ability. *Psychonomic Bulletin & Review*, Volume 17, Issue 4 (August 2010): 479-85

Weiss, Jay M. "Effects Of Coping Responses On Stress." *Journal of Comparative and Physiological Psychology*, Vol 65(2) (Apr 1968), 251-260.

Printed in the United States
By Bookmasters